New York
and
Other Lovers

poems

Also by George Guida

Low Italian: Poems

Letters from Suburbia

The Peasant and the Pen:
Men, Enterprise and the Recovery of Culture
in Italian American Narrative

The Pope Stories

The Pope Play

Pugilistic: Poems

The Sleeping Gulf: Poems

Spectacles of Themselves:
Essays in Italian American Popular Culture and Literature

New York and Other Lovers

poems

by
George Guida

Encircle Publications, LLC
Farmington, Maine USA

New York and Other Lovers ©2020 George Guida

Paperback ISBN-13: 978-1-64599-037-6
e-Book ISBN-13: 978-1-64599-038-3
Kindle ISBN-13: 978-1-64599-039-0

All rights reserved. No part of this book may be reproduced in any form by any mechanical or electronic means including storage and retrieval systems without express written permission in writing from the publisher. Brief passages may be quoted in review. Rights to individual poems and essays remain with authors.

Editor: Cynthia Brackett-Vincent
Book and book cover design: Eddie Vincent/ENC Graphics Services
Cover Image: Shutterstock.com
Inside artwork: Allie Oliver-Burns
Author photo: Denise Scannell

Sign up for Encircle Publications newsletter and specials
http://eepurl.com/cs8taP

Printing: Walch Publishing, Portland, Maine

Mail Orders, Author Inquiries:
Encircle Publications
PO Box 187
Farmington, ME USA 04938
207-778-0467

Online orders:
encirclepub.com

ACKNOWLEDGMENTS

Thanks to Joel Allegretti, Liz Axelrod, Jan Beatty, Adam Berlin, James Berger, Diane Borsenik, Cynthia Brackett-Vincent, Dan Brodnitz, John Burroughs, Juanita But, Chris Cesare, Peter Covino, Sean Thomas Dougherty, Kate Falvey, Joseph Fasano, Alexander Ferguson, Ava Marie Ferguson, Deborah Ferguson, Orlando Ferguson, Paul Fericano, Monique Ferrell, Jack Foley, Jennifer Franklin, René Fressola, Maria Mazziotti Gillan, Michael Graves, Bradley Guida, Florence Guida, George Guida, Sr., Mary Guida, Nancy Harris, Bill Herman, Joanna Clapps Hermann, William Heyen, Charles Hirsch, Bob Holman, Chuck Joy, Lee Kostrinsky, Gerry LaFemina, Lynn McGee, Donna Masini, Joey Nicoletti, Mark Noonan, Robert Ostrom, Pamela Ouellette, Willie Perdomo, Paulette Peters, Robert Peters, Rowan Ricardo Phillips, Connie Post, Vittoria Repetto, Aidan Ryan, Annette Saddik, Denise Scannell-Guida, Neil Silberblatt, Tim Suermondt, Anthony Tamburri, Bob Timm, Christine Timm, Donna Timm, Anthony Valerio, Thomas Verdillo, Robert Viscusi, George Wallace, Pui Ying Wang, and Cee Williams. And a final thanks to my students, for their creative energy, and to New York City College of Technology and Walden University, for allowing the author to earn a living.

Earlier versions of these poems appear in the following journals: "Dong Dai Moon" in *Asbestos*; "The Outcome" in *Barrow Street*; "The Good People of New York City" on The Italian American Writers Blog; "Hindi Radio God" and "Third" in *Light Trauma*; "Brooklyn is a Brand" in *The Long Island Quarterly*; "Poem to Ginsberg" in *Long Island Sounds 2019: An Anthology of Poetry*; "Death Struggle with the Subway Tavern," "I Don't Want to Live in Manhattan," "I Fall in Love," "Life in the New World," "love riff," "New York again," "Shakespeare in the Park," "A Snowy Day Indoors," "Subway Dark," and "What's Fun and What Isn't" in *Perspectives*; "Brooklyn Absurd" in *The Poetry Hotel*; "Manhattan-Bound F" in *The Place Where We Dwell: Reading and Writing about New York City*; "Manhattan-Bound F" (reprinted) and "He Dovens" in *Token Entry: Poems of the New York Subway*.

for Denise,
for lovers gone or never taken,
and for New York

CONTENTS

I.
A Lover in New York

At Last 3
"Rhythm & Flux," by Allie Oliver-Burns 6
I Fall in Love 7
A Snowy Day Indoors 10
Third 12
love riff 13
Why I am not a homosexual 16
I Miss Lucinda Tantilo 17
The Next Time You Go to Kansas 19
Since that day 21
Re-reading *Ulysses* in Nouveau Troy 23
Instead of Dreaming 24
Shakespeare in the Park 25
Thirty-Eight 26
With Her Pen 28
Urban Prodigal 29
The Bus Tour 30
Brooklyn Absurd 32

II.
New York and Other Lovers

Life in the New World 39
"E-Motion," by Allie Oliver Burns 45
Hindi Radio God 46
Halal Marquee 49

Manhattan-Bound F 51
The School of Prophetic Physicians 53
The American Elms 55
The Good People of New York City 57
What's Fun and What Isn't 59
Dong Dai Moon 62
A Brooklyn Troubadour to His Adulterous Beloved 63
Fair Harbor 67
Island 68
In a café, killing time 70
Death Struggle with the Subway Tavern 71
Subway Dark 73
He Dovens 74
I Don't Want to Live in Manhattan 76
Staten Island Ferry 78
Brooklyn is a Brand 79
New York again 82
San Gimignano 83
The Glory That Was Rome 84
fell 85
The Day I Met Larry Rivers 88
Poem to Ginsberg 90
The Outcome 91
More Than a Feeling 93
The Return of George Guida 96

About the Author 97

I.

A Lover in New York

At Last

He calls to say,
   I'm in love, but too late
      for New Jersey,
for a girl who craves
   long-distance drama.
  It's my mid-life crisis.

           Violins

I don't know about her life
   on the verge of surrender
      to a young bed
      or old easy chair.

  Porgy and Bess-like
on a Brooklyn street,
she stops me dead
and takes my hand to ask,
      What are we doing?

I don't know.

I consult the runes of Etta James,
   in love with a married man
    when she sang,
      my lonely days are over
      and life is just
a poem, shorter than it seems,
her melody, a *spogliarello*,
  a strip tease baring the bloody heart,

  I explain, because she says,
    I love Italians like you,
people who speak their heart.

He says,
    I play the bass
        because the heart beats there.
        She doesn't hear it.
    I love her, but
        it ain't gonna happen.
She's just too young.

    Cellos to the bridge

The three-minute song
    dies a long, slow death.
Separate loves of one life fuse
    in suites, sonatas, mash-ups, fugues.

She says,
    You said you were leaving your wife.
I was.
My bags were packed,
    my heart wrapped up in clover.
Now some musician loves her too.

    We're all married in different ways.

She says,
    I understand.
        What are we doing?

    I don't know.

He uploads a song
    he knows she'll hear,
then tries a poem
    he knows she'll never read.

Just American music
      as Etta (born Jamesetta) said.

He was born in Jersey.
He says,
  I'm forty.
  I have to leave it behind.
      Like heroin. Like refrain.

She kisses me like
      brushing a cymbal,
  touches my graying hair (hers dyed),
says,
  What if they found out?
says,
    You know we can't say things like this
        but let's always do,
like a song pretends
    to cast a spell,
          as a cappella
  Etta holds
      the final note like a promise, then

      Dead Stop

                  Violins

Rhythm & Flux

I Fall in Love

    today
   with you
    today
      with someone else
   with you
      with someone else
   with you
     with her
      with someone else
   with you.

Everyday I fall in love
  with the woman reading
her latest work,
  with the woman at work
giving me orders,
  with the woman asking me
if I'm ready to order yet.
   I fall in love
with the doorman who asks
when I'll open my own business
    and give him work.
  I fall in love
   with the counter girl
who rings up my fat free muffins.
  I fall in love
   with joggers in the park
who mingle their winter vapors
   with mine. I fall in love
  with the taxi driver
who fender clips my ankle.
   I fall in love
   with the aerobics instructor

    who works my abs.
         I fall in love
      with the giant bunny
who hands out flyers
              in Union Square.
         I fall in love
      with that cute cop on 57th.
         I fall in love
      with my state senator.
         in love
      with everyone
who knows not who I am.

This is my problem.
         I fall in love with
            the rug.
         I fall in love with
      my print of Pygmalion and Galatea.
         in love with
            reruns of
   "Great Moments in Superbowl History."
         I fall in love with
      elevator buttons.
         in love with
      the ugly 6th Avenue fountains,
            with
      statues of Bolívar and Mazzini,
      Central Park by night.
         I fall in love with
      commuter train views,
            in love with
      The New York Post.
         I fall in love with
      the Borough of Brooklyn,
      suburban strips malls,
            in love with

a Plymouth Gold Duster,
    with stop signs at dawn.
        I fall in love with
cans of turpentine
          rusting on a stoop.
        I fall in love with
especially stupid dogs
      chasing tennis balls.
       I fall in love with
sunset russeted by smog,
with the sound of windswept trees
in concrete canyons,
with dirt, with sunlight,
with two o'clock, with air,
with darkness, with thought,
with the thought that tomorrow

        I'll fall in love again.

A Snowy Day Indoors

Over cider and cinnamon scones
you raise your parents' country place,
and your lips, as if I could
do anything about them.

I say I have dreamt
        of permanence,
a life of justifying me,
too much, we agree,
as you fondle my soft scarf.

But who would give him up?—
good-looking, well-loved doctor—
for a poorly adjusted word thief?
What kind of life would that be
for cider and scones?

Behind your back it's begun to snow
The warm chest spot you lent
                      turns crystal.
My eyes stay dry.

Yesterday I caught your fever,
when you begged me
        with groans and kisses
to release you from goodbyes.
We gulped gin and tonic
in winter light, cloudless and warm.
You said if only things were different.

Things are different.
It's snowing still, but you're gone.
I run cider through a Sunbeam,

      trying to warm it,
      trying to warm me,
though I know it needs a proper flame,
kettle, cozy, tools of home.

It's a snowy day indoors.
Cold breezes chill our bed,
      my bed without you in it.
You inhabit silken sheets
      miles of snowdrifts distant,
miles of streets between us.
You lie in his arms.
You slip away
to cinnamon scones, a country place.

      And your lips.
      And it snows.
      And I have dreamt of permanence.

Third

All of a sudden on Third I am
tripping in circles without God,
thinking again to phone.

You are stolen by Midtown crowds
fifteen years gone by
before I can shout your name.

I am fumbling through my head
for the number you always change
because I call through time.

Once you left me on Third,
returning to find you
in traitor cityscape.

In a moment on Third
someone else with your smile
disappears in deli daffodils.

On Third the thought again of you
leaves me clinging to a street sign:
No Stopping Anymore

All of a sudden on Third you are
a traffic light, horns, a young girl
whose long hair whispers dying vows.

love riff

I don't believe in love.
I have seen it through the snowflakes
     in the spotlight skyline nimbus.
I have tasted it in overnight hot bagels.
I have heard it in a Coltrane riff.
I have sniffed it in a whiff of late November leaves.
I have felt it on skin unsheathed from flannel.

I don't believe in love.
It wakes me up sweating.
It disturbs my shower.
It undresses my strolls down Broadway.
It sings me to sleep on the A.
It carries me to work down Hudson.
It comes and goes and won't leave me alone.

I don't believe in love,
    although I have said it to whom,
    then forgotten in an hour,
    then taken the word,
        and given it to someone else.
I can't brand love in someone's hide,
so how can I believe?

        I want to hug that basset hound.
        I want to hug my pillow.
        I want to hug you,
                then let go.

I don't believe in love.
        Instead I watch t.v.
        Instead I send email.
        Instead I do laundry.

Instead I drink coffee.
Instead I circle the city,
                    seeking love.

I don't believe love
    has wings, makes me cry alone,
    makes art, starts wars (That's fear),
    descends from heaven,
    reduces fever, induces vomiting,
    floats, stinks, hurts, lives
                    up to its name.

        Every time I spoke it
        I believed the word,
        about a good knish,
        about Mark Twain,
        day games,
        the ocean,
        my father,
        my mother,
        Suzanne, Laureen,
        Lucinda, Deidre,
        Jacqueline, you.
                I believed it every time,
            the word, but

when babies smile and aren't mine,
when the fish are biting,
when a kind hand strokes my hair,
        when the day exists to waste,
        when I feel the rhythm
        and discover
            the perfect drink,
            perfect position,
            perfect view,
            perfect word (not love)

    to say, I don't believe in love,
        I say, No, if
                I have to believe,
       everything but.

Why I am not a homosexual

Hans waits by the doors of the Met,
his clean, white, ruffled shirt
harbormaster's light to ship.
We meet for *espresso* and Turandot,
two poets the day before Valentine's,
knee to knee in row S of a gilded hall
erected for lovers and their grandees.

I am young and handsome,
Hans older, Continental,
with an accent that could say
"You look ravishing, my dear,"
to any man at his own wife's side.
(Our wives have learned to leave us
to our spear side evening pursuits.)

Hans and I could easily be gay,
not to live through marriages
that check our self-importance
at the hallway door, and not to spill
our ink from tyrannies of desks
or launch campaigns in silence
as we legislate to find an art.

I could easily hold Hans' hand
as we settle in for the second act,
and revel in the duet's harmonies.
I could try to forget how my eyes
trace feminine forms on sheets
on screens, on canvas or paper,
on palimpsests called afternoons.

I Miss Lucinda Tantilo

whom I did not love that way.

For twelve years now
I have missed Lucinda
with the chestnut hair
and Italian name
that bored me to smiles
on Central Park South.

I miss the chances
at long-billed children
sand and soil-covered
in a decked back yard.

I miss her family's summer house.

I miss Lucinda,
whose roasts and pies
would be daily killing me
faster than the solitude
of Christmases spent alone,
gifts in a closet next to
photos of our younger selves.

I miss Lucinda,
whose hemline froze
a generation back,
whose thin white arms
squeezed desperate love
from my dark Village soul.

I miss my black tee shirt,
so stark against Lucinda's
linen blouse and jeans,
and dispute-free Sundays
of *The Times* and un-cracked books.

I let her go, because
I didn't love Lucinda.
But then I used to believe
in neighborhoods and baseball
and world peace too.

I miss her saying
years later, when we met again
you owe me more than dinner,
and her recognition then
of the fool who freed her
from the clutches of a prince
who never missed anyone
but himself.

The Next Time You Go to Kansas

The next time you go to Kansas,
remember the subway to Queens.
Two lines take you out,
one to Chinatown, the other home.

I'm home, unless I'm out
for chow mei fun. You're out
with earthen *mole* on your fingertips
in a barren shopping mall.

I've got a faceful of Austin Street,
red and green bunting, menorahs,
empanada mavens, Arab
raconteurs, a frosting of snow,

police sirens, railroad horns,
low-rise, imported clay-tile roofs,
and arrays of the aged in search
of juicy plums and peace.

I hear there's a riverbed
on the edge of Potowotomie.
Don't forget to take me there,
the next time you go to Kansas.

In return I'll show you
unispheres and overlooks,
greenways and stadia,
throngs speaking English

to amuse you by Uzbek bakeries,
Buddha shrines and tiny greens
where men of the steppes
pray to gods of chess.

I love the world like this,
when everyone plays a role,
and more when you come back to it
from Kansas, from that simpler place.

But that's the beauty, isn't it?
How here we help each other
make it look as easy as it's not.
The next time you go to Kansas,

if you don't come home soon,
I'll have to visit Chinatown,
moor the other side of Queens,
since it could float out to sea

in absent days if we forget
to keep our one hard mind on home.

Since that day

you beamed down Broadway
the way we had together
fifteen years before,
I've been trying to think.

Since that day
before jet-born rage
leveled our peace,
I've been trying to think

of you at that café table
and all I hoped
would fill your mind
as you accepted tea,

of how I hoped you thought,
Ageless Splendor and His wife,
I wish I were she, as you would
with perfect grammar say.

That September weekend on the town
while you walked West Side sidewalks
searching for a new place in our old
I wanted to shake off lovers lost,

changes I could say were
like new awnings over entries
where we embraced,
where I wanted to feel

your graying strands between
my fingers, in them brittle years
lost to us and tell you as I did
how your touch made life,

however brief or ceaseless,
worth the sacrifice
of any would-be masterpiece,
of any promise I couldn't keep.

We three fixed in still life
the afternoon painted,
I settled on the theme
of innocence lost, believing

I could recompose you,
through that perfect painter's light
fallen on a scarred gray gutter
above us, leaking counterfeit rain.

That night, with foie gras
and a view of towers'
reflections on the river
and someone else,

I thought of how I would survive
you disappeared down Broadway,
beaming brighter, I hoped,
than the skyline lit by the sun.

Re-Reading *Ulysses* in Nouveau Troy

She took me all rainbowstriped and
streetwashed with my barred designer
soap from Bed and Boudoir. Her warm
marble hands lightscoping towers and quays
I threatened to coat with shea. This wayward
Diana raised trees to great acclaim, come to
the whiplash history of calm, brokered
to gentlestrokes, pen coaxed to obscene acts
of reimbezzlement meted out ostinato.
Any portmanteau in a sturm und drang.
This te deum grew tedious gossipel
goldtinted in the real first estate
overestimated in rebirthing pagan
Wests. She saw the continent
but clandestined her stage.
Doppelshadows in art-framed moonbeckon
dappled down Avenues of Alphabets
and ways broadbacked as slaves
who tunneled the trainsfer of souls from burg
to borough. In half-hole I paid her fair to pre-reside
over seebirds' funerals. S-whoops flapped, beached
wails in a troupe of empathy-headed scholars
turned by dungarees from a warning sun.
She skinned herself an epi-ode to wandering
lusts. Doughty no more, she slipped
a lithesome casket and basked
on a sleighbed of ransomed rock.

Instead of Dreaming

I wonder how you'd torture me
as I drank your hair.
The needle in my spine might be
a question mid-sentence or
a pinch of my fat
as your dancer's body slid against.
Would you swear fealty
to martial arts and sensei lessons
I am too long on reason to pursue?

How would I resist the face
that kills me as I cast it
as the thing to die for
while I weight plate myself to death,
only to realize in our rest
that it is scarred above the eyes
and uneven, with a nose that bows
like a hunter's weapon
and too beautiful for me?

I wonder how you'd please me
after pleasing me so long
my mind had gone so flaccid
it could only think the rhythm
of amateur outdoor tango
on a January night in New York,
so dull I could tease no life
from lines like rows of seeds
you'd force me to plant in the air.

Shakespeare in the Park

I used to love New York and hate the Bard.
Around the great park's lawn the towers rose
above a canopy of leaves like brows
drawn up in furrows meant to silence trysts
with lovelorn Gotham wives and their lost men
who like mad mongers hawked its loveliness.

I once loved youth and sentenced age to walk
the streets of equine misery alone.
On sidewalk benches Hamlet sat with me,
so I could wring from him his slowest leave.
I blinkered eyes for sprints and marathons
of questions begging intrigue, fame and death.

Devoid of sentiment, I parroted
The Tempest's epilogue, but dreamt of sex
instead of life's dull edge. I dreamt of years
to come when I would master Shakespeare's lines
and quote them frequently to paramours
I once believed believed in lovers' dreams.

I used to half–believe in *carpe diem*.
New York was opportunity and fate.
New York gave out a catalog of truths
to memorize and share at later dates.
If homeless cabbies whispered miracles,
they lived as bards in perpetuity.

I never used to wait in line. Today
I waited four hours for Henry the Fifth.
The lives of men are such that they delay,
with wanton touch, strong drink, and games of chance,
the study of a young king's boldest crimes
until the jealous city claims their youth.

Thirty-Eight

November 17th, the day
nature's chloroform begins to act
on New York's nerves:
Oak and locust leaves
carpet sooty streets
like fetid confetti.

I am thirty-eight years old today,
riding the subway to work,
to listen closely only to women
who might help slow my march.

I am thirty-eight years old today.
So is the woman I call
co-worker, and more beautiful
than I, but fundamentalist.
I will forgive her, but
want to bring her back
to the world of years, tell her
how all of us are pagans.

I am thirty-eight years old today
and fresh from a fight with my wife,
the woman whom when I can
I love, as always over
undone dishes, moods, abandoned plans
we made in youth
to steel for the coming on.

I am thirty-eight years old
and guide for students half my age.
A young girl reads her essay aloud:
"Abortion: A True Story."

I am thirty-eight today. My son
would have been twelve, a birthday gift,
would have been everything
I'll never find along this path
to decay and memory
of all we were supposed to be.

With Her Pen

I'm writing this with her pen
and she wants to forgive me but can't
because her pen is emerald,
one of fifteen colors
I painted her apartment
when it was ours.

I know it's her pen because
her name is printed on the clip
like instructions, lest you forget
the way her sky-blue irises
caught the filtered bedroom light
through ivory sailcloth curtains hung
in a fit of belief in children
I might teach to love
their poignant thoughts.

She hovers now between
fact and composition, wakes
to search for this pen, for the book,
for the albums that were hers
I took to remind myself
how he used to brew coffee,
how she used to hear him
trying to keep a morning still,
how the train would rumble them
toward future days in quiet
musing on a country scene.

I'm holding her pen now
like a pillow between aching knees.
It's trying to tell me where she is,
though its ink is not so legible,
not so deep a blue as I recall.

Urban Prodigal

The city skyline mopes, jilted.
The lines of age lead my eyes
to her venerable pocking disease.
I have been foolish to leave her so long
alone at the mercy of arrivistes.

    The city skyline weeps, whipped
    by wrecking ball cat o' nine tails.
    Scars bleed open through her glass veneer.
    I never should have given in to age
    and the lie of life without her changing shape.

        The skyline hides in a corner of herself
        by the river where I let her drown.
        Her blue jowls tremble in the night water's fog.
        The crime stains my hands with disappearing ink
        unused in the writing of our life.

    Her outlines darkened by spent lights
    fade in promises the moon won't make.
    She tucks cold faces into fond remembrance.
    I should have kissed her goodnight for years
    lent to strangers with half-parted seas.

The city skyline never wanted to be touched,
although it was she who gave me hands to lay
on the fallen speaking her nonsense tongue.
I should have known I was touching them all
with fingers still crimsoned by her jagged spine.

The Bus Tour

He spoke of the forty percent
foreign born living in New York.
She comes from Florida. I come
from a Long Island town.

Assimilateds cough up more to sit in traffic
than their grandparents earned in a week.
Caught in the turning lane to the bridge
the cab driver says in Arabic English,
*Thank you for ruining my day, my wife
waits now for me in Sunset Park.*

The expressway keeps us from history,
from outer borough burial mounds
planted with ornamental cherries,
our ancestors' bones and the spent cigarettes
of Eritrean gravediggers.

My son-of-an-immigrant uncle
worked on the World's Fair Unisphere,
smoked Lucky Strikes and died
of leukemia in Queens.
Punjab Automotive marks the site.
Death notices appear in Mandarin.

Back on the bus he says
the Chinese specialize,
while Koreans will do anything.
She and I will do what we can
to live here before we die,
to hang from a white stone ledge
by fingernails, above the scene
we want to call home.

Her name appears to me
on a torn Italian-language sign
next to the *salumeria*.
We read in the free paper,
"Americans are most despised of all,"
but I love her among the Indian
grocers she knows by name.

The Americans we hope to make
will feed the pigeons in broad daylight
beneath the Verrazano Bridge
until one day they inscribe our names
on the Ellis Island wall
in a tour guide's hasty script.

Brooklyn Absurd

Here on a traffic island somebody's chained
a bicycle painted entirely white—
rims, tires, handlebars, frame. Since last September
rogue clowns have terrorized the public.
Is this bike one of theirs, poised for harlequin
getaway? I can picture it now:
variegated legs flung out in full flight,
submarine-sized shoes brushing the wheels
of parked delivery trucks, as the buffoon
hooligan coasts to a Smith Street blur.

At the asphalt junction of Flatbush and Fourth
I've just finished reading "The Absurd,"
by a scholar who studied it for years,
now dead. He worked at Princeton, where
my wife taught seven boarding summers
while researching the other seasons
in Oklahoma, seeking inspiration
from prepping the elite. Now we go
back to celebrate ourselves for mentoring
poor kids who want to escape by bridge.

Before the towers died, shops on Atlantic
sold Middle Eastern foods, Persian rugs,
religious texts, hijabs, burqas, and thobes.
Storefronts with Arabic-lettered signs
survive with their windows bricked up or shrouded
like elders sworn to vows of silence.
Crowding these old heads, smooth-faced emporia
display artisanal teas, cheeses
of the world, rehabilitated armoires,
and hemp-lined underwear. Rising luxury
condos squat on their corpses, while lost

business-suited uncles walk still-veiled wives past
those same delivery trucks en route
to far-flung neighborhoods of detached houses
where their children make Americans.

An old, stool-bound, waffle-coated woman claims
the corner of Bond for everyone
who understands what she doesn't say. She is
not begging exactly, but asking
directions our lives will take, as a worker
approaches from the church's stone steps.
He's refused to crew the job across the way:
a billboard oathing future layouts,
doorman, underground parking, gymnasium.
He smokes as he tells her the story
she could tell herself. A hardhat waves from the hole
like a rescue vessel's fair weather
flag. The sunny city gale blows us
past these islands galleried with art
hung in the manner of old-world salamis.

Further down, the Little Wheel Café on Hoyt
perfumes the block with brewed Beirut gold.
Inside, an olive woman I loved in my youth
returns with date-nut cakes she now knows
I can't live without. She smiles as she passes
my plastic future through an Ipad.
Her obsidian eyes bid this aging coil
adieu, and I turn to face the sun
reflected in a brownstone's double window.
This prism beams on a seat between cold heat
pipe and two women speaking Chinese
characters etched in the next table's would-be
jazz musicians' foreheads as they plot
the siege of a small Jersey town. Behind them
a jar of agave sweetens us.

Outside the leaded window new construction
rises for citizens the people
streaming by are sure to become a decade
hence when they stop swearing the powers
that be continue to see the need for them
to do work machines can do in half
the time. A high-rise garage on Livingston
reveals that *Life is a fight for life.*
Close read manholes, light posts, confetti showers,
comic books, pretzel salt, elections
to signify the city's furious speech.
Whose hands should passersby shake? Jumpsuits
polish twelve-foot-high bronze department store doors
while sport coats board a window-barred bus.
Meter maids translate tickets into Sanskrit.

I choose a path, as a squad car sits
idling curbside by the erstwhile Board of Ed.
The bureau's moved to a borough
we can ignore. The renovated building
houses young techies from private schools.
The cop in the cruiser doesn't mind so much
if the influx means better lunches.
Anyway, why would he want to live around
here? Too many immigrants. No peace.
So I decide to turn north, to insist on
distance from the bridge and Manhattan's
skyline on the other side, past the cheap store,
where a pair of shoes could always save
a sorry career, where a gyro vendor
and botanicals peddler confront
the institute where students in defiant
hoodies cluster near a brick building
marked for the latest round of demolition.
The master plan's on nyc.gov.

The City and the Borough and the Mayor
and the Council all have master plans,
but the bagel shop on Fulton has pizza.
Even masters need their solid meals
to survive another day. The office-bound
green space placed on the next super-block
supports a café called La Defense, which sells
pastries in shapes of corporations.
I don't dare eat them, but I do drink coffee
called *Louisiane*. I wish I could
afford it more often, but then I wish too
the pigeons perched in the rowed locusts
were peacocks. Brooklyn has lost its strut. I've heard
the main museum here could have been
the largest in the world, if the foreigners
hadn't arrived when they did. But that
history lies miles away. Closer lie
the criminal court and the mobile
broadcast vans spilling their pretty reporters
like popped magnums of West-Coast Champagne,
sticky and cold, onto the crowded sidewalk
widened for a mogul's zoning deal.

Today's lead story is the stroller derby
from the pre-pre-school to the gourmet
grocery. The celery is certified
organic and makes a great garnish
for selfies. If this scene seems too ponderous
remember what the dead scholar said:
*There is no reason to believe anything
matters.* As Groucho Marx may have quipped,
he had probably just eaten bad tuna
or lost a slap fight in pajamas.
However it was, he must have felt himself
diminished in a fading god's sight,
fading like the taxi's horn as it speeds by

civil court, where a human black eye
barks into her cell, *My baby's not even
in school. He can't even tie his shoes.
And his father don't care,* as passing students
giggle at her mismatched ensemble.
Their laughter infects nearby business suits,
and pretty soon they don't care either.
Why should they when the temperature's this high
and all words vanish into traffic?
As I do, daring to cross a street named Jay,
Chief of the Continental Congress.

In the ugly building I aim to enter,
my wife is crafting plans, not thinking
of how, when we met in another city
over barbecue and beer, I knew
I loved her at first sight because she frowned and
pulled a slip of paper from her purse
and wrote the name of a German theorist
I would never have time to consult.
I told her thank you, and followed her
to a drug store, because we both had grown sick
of cities, and outside our hotel
we stopped to gaze at lights and not to embrace
until the loneliness made us laugh.

II.

New York

and

Other Lovers

Life in the New World

lines written on 9/11/2001

I.

We are westbound,
a background of boroughs,
cell phones held to ears
like the need for psalms.

Rogue planes, jet fuel,
an absence of planted bombs
are rudely interrupting Manhattan.
The World Trade Center, like Godzilla,
absorbs suicide shrapnel,
as office managers' shrieks and roars
charge the September air.

Poets wait eternities to plumb
tragedies laid so bare.
Aboard a bedroom community railroad,
I am only remotely connected.
A woman waving her lifeline
invades my seat, claims
they want everyone out of the city.
I wonder where everyone at risk
of suburban shelter will go.

At a time like this,
what becomes of Brooklyn
between those who see
Manhattan as America,
all conquests and crimes

on display to the world,
and those who see Manhattan as,
of all things, tourist Mecca?

A dusky, turbaned man across the aisle,
a regular commuter in conversation
with a cherry-white woman
dialing like mad to know
if she can have the day off
reads the gentle pen strokes
of a pocket-sized Koran.
At a time like this,
what becomes of him
aboard a middle-class car?
Sudden subject of suspicion,
he asks a question without accent
to the conductor
who suddenly can't remember
the next train out.

Arrived in Brooklyn, I hear
the mayor has ordered us away.
Fleeing, watching the skyline die,
can I fight shadows
for a world that's already gone?
How can I tolerate safety,
when a high school teammate,
fond, forgotten boy,
has known the sensation
of ninety floors trembling beneath,
intimacy with smooth-skinned death?

II.

The twin towers have fallen,
and with them an empire of the senses,

the sense that this New York,
new world, is eternal,
that we will always breathe
the Tuesday air of rhapsodies in blue,
that the subway will always take us home.

Everyone loses some beloved,
some past and future,
when a steel and glass dream falls.

On the Brooklyn streets, crowds gawk
at gray smoke,
at the spectacle of Manhattan,
as they always have,
except in vigil now.
A miles-long cloud ribbons the harbor,
limiting vision to loss.
Two arrogant towers in death
suffocate our innocents,
some spared only by the north wind.
Businessmen klatsched to keep from shaking,
speak of death to immigrants, payback
for crimes we have all committed.

III.

Escaped, beneath a trestle I am lost
in suburban sunlight and siren shadow,
half-witness to death,
to imagined wives and mothers
imploded like skyscrapers
collapsing our memory of peace
in the million pieces
that are each one lost
to plastic explosive anger,
poverty and dire religion.

I am staring at suburban sun,
clinging to faith.
I pray for 100th floor jumpers,
for acrid smoke inhalers,
for sad generations
newly sworn to vengeance.
Safe in my family home, I opine,
the sins of the father,
cross-couch from my own,
retired law enforcer,
warrior by taste,
watching as we watched before
the smart-strafing of secular sons,
the hidden slaughter of daughters,
their misfortune to dream in Arabic
under a different sun,
lost to the blood-lusty cry,
"Bomb them back to the Stone Age."

IV.

We stumble among rubble now,
as poisonous clouds drift out to sea,
where navy vessels steam
through red and black spume,
to rescue us from harm,
though all the harm is done,
every rumble in the distance
a shout for war, an assault
on the ignorant peace of means.

Worst of all is absence:
of towers,
bankers,
secretaries,

firefighters,
Arab brokers,
cops like my father,
and still here
a callous leader chastened,
and we, eastbound, ocean-bound,
finally world-facing,
absent from our former selves.

White soot-covered zombies
of the new millennium,
we wash our hands like Pilate,
comprehend televised images
like special effects,
jumbo jets, American and United,
annihilating our national dream.

V.

We live now in a land
of detectors and snarling dogs,
cavity searches and pat-downs.
We are the old world reborn.
The new has drifted beyond
serene skies and putrid clouds.
We speak of death as one
with attack amnesia
might speak of Hawaii.

We live now with
King Kong, the primate,
beating his chest atop
the Empire State still upright
in the distance, an illusion
of another American time.

We cling to that tower
through t. v. screens,
as heroes and beasts in agony,
conscious of our sense
that once we had a home.

E-Motion

Hindi Radio God

drive my cab all night long
listen for signals
voice of voices
the Hindi Radio God

    ABRA LOOB KAJANI

Hindi Radio God
lost in the Brooklyn static
Hindi Radio God
a dollar-fifty the first eighth mile
Hindi Radio God

onward runs the meter
Hindi
cherry air freshener
Radio God
beads on my seat
Hindi Radio
beads on my rearview
God

voices voices
distant nations
incantations
or directions
from Penn Station
in borough static
conflagration

doomed sienna comets sonar
where the Radio God?

Boom Boom

RAJAN HASUNI

commands the Hindi Radio God
voices suffer unto him
Hindi Radio God
who pulls me through the fear of night
and white and children children

Hindi Hindi Hindi Hindi
God God God
Hindi Radio Radio Radio
Radio Radio God
God Oh Hindi Hindi God
Hindi Radio God Hindi
God Oh God Oh Hindi Radio
Radio Hindi God

God-God
Radio Radio Radio Radio Radio
Radio God
Hindi God Radio God
Radio Hindi Hindi God
God Radio Hindi Radio
Hindi Hindi God

SALEM ALUD JALILE

fear not above the park my heart
fear not above the God
sing Lincoln Tunnel Holland Tunnel
Hindi God God
sing Verrazano Narrows
and the narrows of my soul
sing Brooklyn-Queens Expressway
under God's remote control
wireless wireless radio boy
Hindi subject man

wireless Hindi boymangod
Radio Radio man

oh passenger my passenger
I take you where I can
I might I would I should I must
nothing more than Radio man
Radio Radio Radio man
God God God

steering wheel is Hindi
from the windshield wiper God
the Hindi God the Hindi God
the Radio Radio Hindi God
the God the Hindi God God Radio
Radio God the Radio God
the Hindi Radio God God God
the Radio Hindi God

    ASHREF KALAN MURUKA

I
sing Hindi Radio God

Halal Marquee

The whole world sings
Kebab with Rice
Kebab with Rice
All Day Best Price
Falafel Platter
Falafel Platter
Shawarma, Shawarma, Shawarma

Spices summon you to carts
Hammered silver Samarkand
Swear allegiance to East and West
Manichaean pita torn and stuffed
Lamb or Hummus
Lamb or Hummus
Board of Health Certificate
Eastern Paper, Western Print
Syob and Sogd
Tigris, Euphrates
Karun and Murat
Cola flowing from a hidden source
Ice Cold, One Dollar
Ice Cold, One Dollar

Here you are
And there you go
The smoke is clouds of peace
Clouds that please
Halal, Halal, Halal
Tiny suns flash tiny prayers
Tahini, Tahini, Tahini
Try the babaganoush
Spell it this way
Spell it that

It only matters how you eat
Tabouleh, Dolma, Kafta, Fattoush
All day until the darkness comes
Then we pray
Halal, Halal, Halal
Salaam, Salaam
My Friend, Salaam

Manhattan-Bound F

In Queens, before the crowds
when the train is mine
to sit and dream, I dream
a life for scattered riders
with dog-eared books
of old world laws
which seem no longer to apply.

I dream of sober days
and drunken nights alone
aboard this eight-car lifeline
to nowhere with its silver teeth
bared to all who challenge peace.

What is a dream leaving Queens?
Is it the loss of place
for the genuine we call upon
in hours of need? Is it
a sleepy-eyed Korean girl
with doe-eyed beau
caressing spoken characters
from her throat? No.

In Queens, before the crowds
I bare my ambitious soul.
Oh, that I believe, for all
the migrants' bygone gardens,
my words will ride the rails
to the places where
we (never) want to go.

In the run of good souls
aboard the F train

no one dreams of politicians.
No one dreams
of the F train home
beneath the East River,
its history of orphans
and eels like God's tongues
ground to muck on the bridges' feet.

Aboard the F train, riders
thumb their mental cookbooks
for ways to prepare soldiers
of their countries' dirty wars
for the new-world table. Sacrifice
feeds the mainland dogs
who prowl the fringe of Queens
as though its people were the first.

In Queens freedom is all
your father wanted to deny
existence. The lone riders
watch for unattended bags
as the train pulls into Roosevelt.
In Queens the tabloids militate
against the contemplated life
of stonings and feasts.

The School of Prophetic Physicians

Who swears by this cabal
of robed Brooklyn billboard reverends
beneath whom brown glue congeals

through winters until paper hummocks
twist the holy faces southward
toward the Plains where

university deans dole out
painful honors to politicians,
salesmen, spirit singers shuffling

across the stage, about to end
their lives? And why do they
belong on May-green meadows

we strolled honeysuckled, Shasta-daisied,
north of the stadium, south
of the state where I came to find

you in someone else, another
land-grant school pinned with oaks,
pimped with parapets, mock-history

too brief for diagnosis?
You're a doctor now, but not
a physician or meta one

who bleeds my letting go
of moments in topsy-turvy
Turkish coffee mud mugs,

a life upended by decisions

the size of linemen, powerful
as preachers' words fallen

letter by iron letter
from Brooklyn brick black-top roofs
soon to limn new luxury condo

immigrant lives, from towns like
many you've left behind, we've left
alone in these cities raising crystal

walls to grassy pain we know
will prophesy our doom
in birth defects and plans

for houses, trips consuming us
like students on gold-tasseled binges
in bars where fortunetellers sip.

I foresee the day brick walls
give way to naked clergymen,
frocks cast to gutters

of mirrored streets that end
at feet of brown bulkheads,
carpeted tomb-beds we knew

as memorials. As we rise,
the horizon dips. I love
the sequined coat folded over

your helm or creaky bassinette
that steers us toward sleep
to hymns we'd like to sing

to someday soon forget.

The American Elms

The city's grown frail
so touch can only do it harm.
I've forgotten which city I mean.

But here is the final stand of American elms,
where an old man's tee shirt loves New York,
while a young man's sexes it to death,
and everyone looks up the elms' grass skirt.

Like all ads our clothing's lied.
We bellow the city's name in cotton,
Stanley Kowalski volume, yet
Tennessee Williams will die again.

I'd like to parade lost names
down ruined Esplanade,
but most are gathered on Broadway,
waiting to leave the second line.

Gangs would steal them,
if they didn't fear names the way
Mardi Gras tribes fear silent nights,
the way we, tom-toms beating loss.

Here I am sad in Central Park,
unsure of tickets,
foggy on plot,
doubtful of tragedy,

sitting again in that club
on Congo Square, in the Marigny,
loose-jointed drunks at our flank,
on sax a lanky teenaged Creole.

When the washboard comes my way
I strafe a streetcar rhythm
toward Cemetery Number Two,
the smell of camellia on us like sin.

The Spanish moss has drifted
from jazz's tomb, like a lover's arms
on the artist's walk, is begging now
to drape it over unimagined boughs
of these lonesome American elms.

The Good People of New York City

They did not get a good night's sleep,
but woke to blades of island
sun through dirty blinds.

The good people of New York City
sit in a coffee shop, sipping joe
from a chipped ceramic mug
and hum the latest song about
making it in New York City.

Look, there, the good people of New York
are reading tabloids at the corner stand.
For a minute they've forgotten
how to pay, but look again,
they're kibitzing now with the clerk
in the red flannel vest.

The good people of New York City
often take the subway
but today have decided to walk.
It's just a few blocks to the florist
and already the rain has stopped.

They're wearing tennis shoes
but no sunglasses, since
they don't mind being recognized.

The good people of New York
are walking through the park
to their favorite stand of linden trees,
where they unwrap knishes
while ducks splash down.

Look, the good people of New York
have fallen asleep in the grass.
They dream of being tourists
at the Statue of Liberty's feet,
but wake up sure they'll never go.

Back home our good people recline
on fire escapes and sketch the street.
They'd head to the bodega for beer,
but it's Sunday. Not that it's closed.
It's just they need their wits, enough
to talk about the sunset over Jersey.

Then the Chihuahuas will need their walks
and the good people of New York
will have to call their mothers
to let them know that life is not
what they thought when they used to be
the good people of everywhere else.

What's Fun and What Isn't

Moss-green walls of dental day spas
glow like chlorophyll
of doctors' ficus trees

abandoned on rooftop patios
where children's pails lie strewn,
puce cockles on a wintry beach.

Satellites beam heat and radio waves
to paneled family minivans where
no one watches porn on tiny screens.

If you're looking for kicks,
they're hidden in Greenway Park,
where dogs and profiteers fear to tread.

New pet stores are raffling
canine body armor meant for
rows with wild boar,

worn on haute Queens streets
like pain coats, with the sheepish eyes
and snouts of battlefield dead.

Christmas bunting's up not to see
the Avenue of Redundant Boutiques
and Boulevard of Peaceful Weekends.

The Street hosts five cell phone showrooms,
so we can always be reached,
so we can work all the time, like

the city's water tunnels, like

power lines, like
motion-sensor spotlights.

The God of Sports Clubs broadcasts
Brazilian dance-hall queens
and neo-punk, magenta-dyed dryer pros

with ads for ten-minute ab torture,
trap trick, bi rip, hammy lift, glute pump,
and the popular pec pop.

Everybody works for the weekend house,
where a dozen glossy home-improvement tomes
lie stacked like bricks of wishful thinking,

where pleasure is a perfect record
of draining the pipes for hard freezes,
though should we forget,

the plumber in newly painted truck
will bring the beer, and gift
mini-toilet key chains to the kids we made

so they could watch those educational cartoons.
We never liked playing catch,
and dollhouses just kill trees.

¿Cuál es la fecha de hoy?
Those are the Spanish lessons we all take,
unless we're studying English on weekends,

baring our glistening torsos other days.
Is there any other way
to have them glisten so?
On weekends we pray

over mega-church guitars,
or live stream for brethren.

We belong to a Big Team,
as on Field Day. We sack race
down the nave, play tug-of-war

along the transept,
competitively pie-eat in the apse,
call out bingo from the benches,

as at the pulpit our leaders pin ribbons,
some for participation,
some for victory.
When we approach for rewards,
we say all glory to God
until someone believes us,

like the game we played as children:
truth, dare, consequence,
promise, or repeat.

Dong Dai Moon

Here in Flushing we find

      the Dong Dai Moon Total Store

where everything is,
    including your broken heart,
        discovered in San Francisco,
           abandoned in a woman's wonton soup.

You had abandoned hope,
    have recovered it
        on the shelves of Dong Dai Moon
           near a creek called a bay
           in a borough called Queens
           in a language called Chinese

    you understand by habit, and how to find
    behind the painted porcelain palace dogs
        what you must one day leave behind

    again, a wind-up memory of your time here,
        self consigned to Dong Dai Moon,
           more than you could bear.

Beyond this commerce people
    speak their purchased secrets
    for simple mornings on a country porch,
        their faces like scents of loose teas
        vanished from the Total Store
           as it will be
                after you.

A Brooklyn Troubadour
to His Adulterous Beloved

I. Brooklyn Promenade

Too much, not enough of a good sting:
Towers sing, Stay where you are!
The city knows everything.
We can not unzip the river
  to crawl inside.

Streetlamp aureolae ring this cave
on wheels that ride
the Brooklyn street tide shoreward
  or toward the Promenade.

It's odd so many feet
don't know their heading
at midnight when arms cling
to each other, desperate
to borrow from the borough
  a life run backward.

    Deliver us sinners
to the thousand churches.
    Deliver us
to chapels of consummation.
    Summon us
from this boardwalk,
this catwalk, this sleepwalk,
to a cloister of resolve.

Whisper in my ear,
this postcard is a promise,
this drama's premise won't sustain

      a single message.
On stage now we are crawling
      for the wings.

The sweet butterflies of night
press themselves
in books of billet-doux.
For the moment neither of us reads
this romance tongue that spoken frees
      a two-room tombful
      of canaries.

II. Brooklyn Bard

Walk with me, Sally McBride
in a heaven of parallels,
for the lines stretch long.

Sing dead songs, Sally McBride
from your window of wishes
that gliss down upon.

Sally McBride, Sally McBride,
my winter cloak to wrap you in acts
against the bluster of facts.

What's in a name? Sally McBride,
what's the mark on your ever-smooth cheek?
The trick, you say, lies not in the read.

Softly, Sally, Sally McBride,
descend with silver water.
I live to return your speech.

Sally McBride, your two tails

fast to a tree, I tell you,
the gale will die with the storm.

Sally McBride by the sea,
this harbor lies openly
to an ocean of close-knit brows.

Sally McBride, the windjammer prow
at avenue ease will whistle,
you whistle, a lamster air.

Sally, come walk with me, Sally McBride,
over concrete pastures,
past sickle cells of mneme.

Sally McBride, free you me
of banquets, barons, boroughs.
Free me you to dally by your side.

III. Brooklyn Alba

"You, lover, blink at the sun,
      shield your eyes
        from Brooklyn's questioning dawn
as it defrocks the night,
to summon slaves
          to sunrise."

"And lover, you have wound both feet
   in sheets meant to cover.
     This is no Thirteenth Century,
   no honor to defend,
no stake at which to burn.

     You can ride the subway home
at sunrise."

"You, lover, you, I serenade
    your guarded window,
    but only by night will you hear
    strains, chains will you hear
    rattle, but always unchained
upon sunrise."

"And you, lover, there in chains
    tintinnabulate streets,
        rumble tunnels at dawn.
A story guides your step
across a place, a palimpsest,
a denouement
to untie sunrise."

      "We must part now, we must part.
The way to Brooklyn lies far too long,
    the way home longer still."
Sing, lover, to the many winds,
lest we forget the two-room tune,
the window above us
    reflecting the moon,
    thrown open to welcome
our sunrise."

Fair Harbor

Yes, we are ships, and yes, this is a sea
of yeses. We are eating scones at noon
and no one is your lover, hand on knee,
horizon set, and you'll be eighty soon.
Helen, here in Queens how light you sigh
at thoughts of whys you never could disown.
A sea of nos, a phony cup of chai
don't drown the young woman of flesh and bone
your brown eyes revive. The wind would agree,
if you could hear its promised baritone.
You ordered coffee, but they brought you tea,
whose steeping storm convinced you to atone,
then brought a tarnished spoon to row your skiff
back to the harbored schooner bound for if.

Island

We moved to a run-down townhouse
holding pen, two rooms, eight by ten,
exposed brick wall and salvaged photos of
  abandoned loves.

When your marriage didn't take,
you blinked too fast and found yourself
shopping the mall for a fake wood futon
  and flakeboard bookshelves.

We stood on the threshold
of closing on a dog-friendly
three-bedroom with an oak-tree
  view of an old-age home.

You blessed our September
yard-party union, as your wife sat alone
on a white glider, harkening back
  to her gown and the hall's Napoleons.

Your wedding night she'd slept on a chair
while you'd played poker on the hotel stairs.
Between you grew a golf course
  and weekends of divorce.

You drove us to the mall for picture frames,
electrostatic mops. You swore
she'd tried. You were the one to blame.
  We loved you still and didn't care.

You asked the co-op's asking price
and didn't hear the answer.
Another friend who sailed through life alone

in a downtown walk-up
  ship's cabin next week will marry

a woman twenty years too young. She
will live in a ten-room Dutch colonial. He
will sail out through the Narrows
  in a toy boat bound for Atlantis.

In a café, killing time,

you find nothing done.

The music breathes too loud,
the counter orders fill in shouts.

A pretty young boy is
casting grasping eyes your way.

On the sidewalk an endless cast
of unknowns lead their dogs and kids

on glacial rounds, while purpose rests
with joggers, buses, Ubers and bikes.

For you with dreams and magazines,
losing this hour is art as hard

to master as what happens now
or promises never to happen at all.

Death Struggle
with the Subway Tavern

Neither of us has stopped breathing
for decades. I watch each time I wander past
Lexington and 60th, for its neon flicker,
for fewer like me to stagger from its door
into the sidewalk night.

It watches me every year
more slowly loping toward a train
that somehow gets me home.
It waits for me to slip,
fall prey to younger strays.

Each time I pass, I think,
How can it be still there?
squeezed between
the smoked glass office
and renovated brownstone.
But there it is in all
its pink and blueness,
gin and beerness,
daring me to walk the avenue
another twenty years.

Some year soon I'll step inside,
smash its steins and highballs,
pour acid on its varnished oak,
and cripple its folk with blarney.
Or it will poison me
with treacly liqueurs,
pour them down my throat
until my legs give way, until
I fall to a sloe-eyed denizen

who'll make me forget my name.
Each year I wander closer, later.
Each year I mumble louder, lower
    than the neon's hum,
        the bouncer's phlegmy cough,
        and the laughter from deep inside.

Subway Dark

        Lights are dead inside. We sit
        apart at folded crosses, questions
        set to pop, as bulbs
        inside a tunnel, as here
        or here swirl shadows

    faces shadows arms to clutch

    keys pens conceptions

all our would-be thrusts
through space, through shadow
    through ourselves
    for dark defense

He Dovens

He dovens
while I don't
on this train
where no book
ever hints
what to think.
You think
at first
he bobs
like the tap
of a foot
by the strappers
overhanging
the tonsure,
the tappers
who signal
above where
the gaggles
of Chassids
plan Sabbath
by shuls,
to sing songs
that call
to the dovener,
you,
whose tune,
vaguely sounds
like "Oh,
Susannah"
or else
"Get Happy"
which critics
insist

derive from
rabbinical
chant.
What goy
can impugn?

Or it could be
the subway chimes
of different lines
like history notes
on tuning forks
that call the flock
at fasting time
when hunger shows
in deep-set eyes
as he rocks himself
too high in soul
to read.

I Don't Want to Live
in Manhattan

You can keep it
and your stockbroker brick-oven pizza.
I'll take steel-cart shwarma and falafel
near the El.

Keep the memories
of Third Avenue. I'll live in Queens
or Brooklyn sin, divorced from towers
that drew my youth,

make sweet, long love
on papery sheets to a dark-skinned girl
who only speaks the English tongue
for strangers.

I know all about
the condos with views of Central Park.
On a clear day, you can see New Jersey.
On a clear day, I can see

the wi-fi laundromat,
the calling card cafés along the boulevard,
and undergraduate peregrines
to this other city.

I can smell the *maduros*
frying, too. So keep your marble lobbies,
oak bars, copper ceilings, silver-handled
bathroom tip jars,

while I relieve myself
by the brown rat can against the mustard tile,

near the muddy, used-condom track bed
of my far-flung terminal.

Staten Island Ferry

The boat, named for a long-dead bureaucrat,
chugs from its moorings and swings
around brown pilings toward St. George,
ignoring the Brooklyn Bridge.
Two cops swagger down an aisle,
watching for which group—
Italians, Blacks, Latinos,
renegade Russian émigrés—
will be the first to reach their baggies down
to snag an ounce of sea
to make the steeples of Old New York
fade behind walls of marble and steel,
and fix us for a moment,
then slip from sight and vanish
into watery flight
beside the ancient copper gown.

Brooklyn is a Brand

I have to explain
to my Brooklyn
relations
buried alive
with handful upon
handful of dust
that Brooklyn is
behind besieged brick
brownstones darkened
windows tagged
Hands Off My Home
Brooklyn is
kids on the block
named Shorty and Sam
and Mad Dog and Moise'
and Russ-D with tongues
stuck out at you
and never quite the same
since they got jumped
Brooklyn went
and came back
Brooklyn is a brand
(fast-talking)
Brooklyn Fare
Brooklyn Books
Brooklyn Wireless
Brooklyn Body
Brooklyn Hair
No names that speak
people who were
who are. Brooklyn
is a brand Brooklyn
is an indie film

about Brooklyn
directed by
someone who left
before high school
with beat clothes
and a ledger
You can wear
your Brooklyn
baseball cap
turned backwards
toward air-brushed
Nineteen Fifty-Five
Brooklyn Sundae
Brooklyn Rail
Brooklyn Business
Improvement District
Yo Brooklyn
Where you at?
Black Brooklyn
is a brand
The Brooklyn Museum
sells keychains and pins
Three million people
swallow the granite
dust of inscribed
Dutch names
Brooklyn hip
Brooklyn cool
Brooklyn soul
the Bridge walk
listed as must-do
Brooklyn is a tattoo
and a sign:
Now Leaving Brooklyn—
Fuhgeddaboutit
It's the place

it's told to be
the word on the street
you didn't have to shout
the handbill carts
where the mob was
Brooklyn is
a brand Brooklyn
is the unfurnished
room in the high-rise
full of echoes
empty of names
is everyone

New York again

on Valentine's Day I love
what gilded age collectors
thought was Europe
re-chiseled in American bedrock
walls avenues I appreciate
like magnums of vintage water
wash my palate with polished marble
pillars on which I rest
my hope of you in stride
down one of these sidewalks
past brass plaques embedded
we read in our history
books of New York and why
we need, you and I
this walk again

San Gimignano

Fourteen keeps lurch skyward,
aspiring to New York.
        The Empire State Building
viewed from an office window
announces, This is mine,
this steel, glass, and concrete
praise to self, and in the background
        God.
In its windows the granite blocks
of towers and families
who, erecting them, claimed
that they could all
but die.
    In the sense
that our bus drops us there
to compare, they live.
We compare our New World keep
to nothing that survives,
selling it, piece by piece,
to jousting interests,
renaming it for royals,
deflecting eyes from
dun block fissures
quarried of prayer
the *Commune* bathes
in soft spotlight,
leaves off anointing
        Skyline

The Glory That Was Rome

The kick line, kick line, kick line
sends us in flight above
the Radio City stage.
The greatness of that age gone by
rumbles, twinkles the orchestra pit
with mechanized confetti.
Triangles tink the final notes
of soldier girls' tin grins.

It's beginning to look a lot like Christmas
past, the pageant of glory days
that makes gray parents swoon
to the majestic swing of youth.
Again we are Christian,
this Deco hall our church.
For the moment, the sea of white
confines the Levantine third act
to the grand souks, boutiques,
and late-day shish-kebab stands.

We gape at the moribund
Sugarplum Fairies, skaters
ascended from nether Rockefeller,
and anthropomorphized
snowmen gliding across
a collective conscience of ice.

`fell`

moments before he
  was fishing pockets
    for change for tickets for the 7:19
moments after he
  had eaten dinner, going on
    about a raise and vacation time
      he thought he might have earned by
    putting just a few more hours in
  at the office each week, he said
to his wife swizzling
a gin fizz, his wife not
  paying attention, he not really either
    and he thought again about
      this weekend, two days together,
    the 7:19 away from this and
  the work he wouldn't get done and
the thinking he wouldn't do and
the Knicks' playoff chances and
  the waitress's and his wife's
    legs and maybe a threesome,
      but she would never go for that
    and do I still make her
  come and do I still smell
o.k. after a long day
at the office, running
  around, because it never seems
    to end, but at least lunch
      was better than usual, no hot dogs,
    spinach pie the way George's mother
  used to make us kids before
this job which never
seemed right for me because
  I wonder if I'm doing it

       right, if I ever
       did or should I
wonder about that now when I have
  a train to catch and we need to
spend time, my wife
and I, but now we have to
  pay the tab and go, because
      these trains run on time and I
          don't and we may not have many
      more weekends away or even
  drinks if Monday I'm fired, then I
won't know what
to do, since I've never done
  anything and my wife
      only works when she
          wants, but I can't believe I'm
      worrying about this now, because
      what good will it do me when
  all I want to do is see
the sunset and listen
to the ocean and touch
  my wife and be happy,
     and kids, though I'm not
          sure, so let's catch the train,
      he thought and pulled his wife
  across the street to the terminal
doors where he smiled at a cop and
thought about what they would
      eat while he could still
          afford it or if eventually
              they would starve to death, because
          he had failed, he thought and watched
  the big clock on the kiosk, taking the first
step down the stairs, and
seeing just before a little girl
     running, trying to keep up

with her parents running
     for the 7:19, and another step
before wondering, until the terminal
     heaved sideways, upside
          down, and away
               from his wife,
                    and began to feel,
                       step by step,
                          the pain

The Day I Met Larry Rivers

he couched himself in fresh-fucked art bunny
as the door of his living room lift
snapped open and out popped
two more awash in acrylics.

The day I met Larry Rivers

through Arnold, a male voice sobbed
at his still hawk profile in oil
on canvas, his pastiche lips,
sounds translated through monkey
lackeys leaning on Fourteenth Street.

The day I met Larry Rivers I realized

if you endure New York for long enough
you meet Larry Rivers, New York
where he said to bang a person
is to know a person.

The day I realized I met Larry Rivers

I wondered how that would change my life,
what he had to do with the dead
painters and poets, cats and chicks
in black and sometimes the Hamptons
and now his apartment with a copy
of "Washington Crossing the Delaware."

The day I met Larry

I was typing cuts and pastes
of his life through Arnold,

was wondering if I might be too late
to meet De Koonings and Pollocks,
Freilichers, O'Haras, Kochs, those
who had them at the pre-film Chelsea,
before the quiet of laptops
and calls to Utah for support.

The day Larry Rivers met Me

he grunted, belted back another bourbon,
buried his face in bunny,
told Arnold it might be nice
to leave the old apartment
for a stroll downtown, past
the many young people
aging through him, handed me
his empty, named it
through reedy lip belch,
"Memento."

Poem to Ginsberg

I swore that writing to your name would be
worse than saying, as I have, we knew each other.
I never liked it when their friends or, even worse,
acquaintances like me penned dead literati.

But there you are, at a cocktail party,
caged in a suit, perched on a riser
high above New York, with younger me
watching how you faced a wall of glass,

yourself, and a silent city from that state.
And what could I do? And what now?
when your gaze tried to hold so much
a young acquaintance could never know.

And there you were in your apartment,
near rows of chunky book shelves
stolen from library stacks. And in fact
your name mattered only

because you'd stolen everything
we wanted more than we understood.

The Outcome

to Frank O'Hara

In the Seventies you would have sat
with Warhol movie stars
you wanted to be.

Your great head eclipsing
late news lenses, disco
would never have been your bag.

You would have lost to academe,
been invited
and invited.

AIDS would not have touched you,
would not have written you a poem
to undo a Pope or President.

You would have been the old queen
with his platitudes, the one who said
the grass sings poetry.

You would be living in New Mexico,
if New Mexico had a city.
Is there a condo for old poets?

The alcohol would have killed you
no matter what, no matter you
were humming Stravinsky

on the beach that night,
the tune we would have heard
in your latest interview.

Painters, museums, ballet:
You would not have attended.
I'm done with it all,

I can hear you say,
with exact times of day,
through with clouds and streetscapes.

A poem about a cloud?
Ridiculous. Really,
Who do you think I am?

More Than a Feeling

Listening in a bathtub
to Boston riffing Bach
on bass and B-3 organ,
I'm back last night with the boys
all pushing forty in a dive bar
where a drunk yelled Italian
mulagnan' to Dan, who thought
he was a blurred hit man.

It's been such a long time.
And here comes Brad Delp
over high G with suds.
And I want to lay down rhythm
but might as well think of Lee's
"No way!" as I give my answer
to Funniest Movie Scene ever?
No way to "Rock and Roll Band,"
corniest tune ever written
I love in spite of myself,
whom I still see wailing
the riff at twenty-five
on a guitar I still can't play.

Then "Smokin'," straight-ahead
roomful of cheap cigars,
soggy wontons, and bottled beer
that still had me poisoned
when I woke up today at noon,
alone in a bed my wife's deserted.
A message I read in curtained sunlight:
Miss you. Can't wait for New York.
Last night in New York City.
I don't want to get carried away

or maybe that's it when you're sliding
down Eighth Avenue, middle-aged,
to Chris's place with
tattooed temptress roommates
and the boarder's cats.
There was something about you,
Baby, don't yell
about feline incursions.
We'll take care of everything.
It's cool. Time's dead.
We stopped it at 1:02 a.m.,
Monday, December 27th.
Year doesn't matter.
No tsunamis
in your morning news.

Before my eyes, the water
shrivels my skin, but God,
what a perfect final chord.
Dan said a lot was perfect
when we shared twenty.
Now he reads my mind:
Boston for Christmas.
Old notes hang together,
bare chords out front.
We just gotta get loose,
because what do they call us now?
How much Puccini can we do?

Lee mentioned mushrooms,
and maybe that's the way
to kill our families
once and for all.
I'd visit them tonight, but
I don't want to make excuses.
When this electric's done,

I don't want to lie.
The band fades in again
and I re-start the clock.

I forgot everyone's a scribe
if he's not a rocker.
Each old boy's at home,
after snow and midtown traffic,
with his pen and treble clef,
his tubful of tepid water
and headful of riffs, singing
All I, all I want is…

The Return of George Guida

George Guida announces, *I'm back, New York!* Construction cranes pirouette,
as all the silence he's left behind rings in his ears like a zombie payphone
at a subway stop. He's finally acceded to the concept of youth
as culture club he can no longer join. He has aged to concrete.
The Brooklyn Bridge is no longer a springboard, but a bed.
He lies down because he isn't tired. His eyes are open wide,
to take in gray steam from the sidewalk grate and black dust
from the unswept stoops. Welcome back, calls the little girl growing up
here, knowing lobbies as yards, the myth beginning again.
He's cleansing himself in a cramped bathroom's miniature sink,
in a railroad apartment's kitchen tub, on a fire escape in the rain.

He's as back as a gentrified block in Brooklyn. You can find him at lunch
on the swings by the softball fields. The pigeons have missed him
and come cooing. He buys a knish and searches for *The Daily News*,
for two-word headlines. The bridges are all alight. The inbound traffic
is a symphony he conducts. A homeless woman on the steps
spots him and shouts that she is home. From Houston to Harlem
he's forgiven. The Bronx knows he left in haste. He scales a tower
and sings to Staten Island. An old man on a Broadway bench is telling him
how lucky they both are. You don't have to be a New Yorker to understand.
You just wait for the bus. You say hello to the people who ignore you
as they pass. And the street takes you in. And just like that, you're alive.

About the Author

George Guida is the author of nine books, including *The Pope Stories and Other Tales of Troubled Times* and five collections of poems: the first edition of *New York and Other Lovers, Low Italian, Pugilistic, The Sleeping Gulf,* and the forthcoming *Zen of Pop*. He lives and works in different parts of New York State, and teaches writing, literature and cultural studies at New York City College of Technology. Visit georgeguida.wordpress.com.